EVIL FREAKS
(Beyond Gross)
Horrors of a Borderless World

Manual for
Superior Men

A complete theory based on Einstein physics,
Political Psychology, Systems Theory
and Archetypal Psychiatry.

FORMULA

All success attraction
All disease obstruction
All recovery elimination

You must fast on all three

OBSTRUCTIONS:

People
Habit
Food

EVIL FREAKS

I was different from the beginning and could not adapt to social devices and silly grinning. I was always sided against: the dumbed mob vs. the inconvenient woman with thoughts. They hated the odd girl out in every social arena and I ended up escaping/crying for momma. The pain from being deceived by those closet cannot be expressed. Recognize these social devices keeping you down cuz it's always by clowns wearing crowns.

EVIL
FREAKS
[beyond gross]

KAREN
KELLOCK

EVIL FREAKS

EVIL FREAKS HUMILIATE
LIBERALS CODDLE CRIMINALS
TRIGGERED SHAME
FREEZING WITH INVASION
KNOW/OWN YOUR FEELINGS
STAND UP FOR YOURSELF
IMPOSING INGRATES
BOUNDARIES HAVE CONSEQUENCES
THEY LIKE THE AGREABLE
BOUNDARY BLOCKERS
BOUNDARIES AND RED FLAGS
BEST FRIEND AND HUSBANDS
WOMEN DON'T HAVE BEST FRIENDS
SEPARATE YE
TWO STATES: GRATING OR HUMMING
GOD TOOK EM ALL OUT
ESCAPE THE GROSS GUY
SHAME FOR OLD ASSOCIATIONS
THE UNAPPRECIATED GOOD HUSBAND
IT'S HARD TO FORGET IT ALL
SELF-DISCOVERY
FEMINIST BACKLASH
DON'T HEX NEW SYSTEMS
PHASE TWO: HOOK HER ON HIM
TOXIC MASCULINITY

EVIL FREAKS

EVIL FREAKS

NARCISSISTIC INJURY
TO THE LOVE ADDICT
NECESSARY VULNERABILITY
SOCIAL PSYCH: CONTAGIOUS HATE
SMALL TOWN SCAPEGOATISM
WOMEN THE BEST PRISON GUARDS
TRANSCEND EARLY RESISTANCES
THEY TURN ON ALLIES EASILY
ANGER STYLES THE INDICATOR
PASSIVE AGGRESSIVE DIRT BALLS
I HATED THEIR COMPANY
LOW TRUST LEVELS
BEGINNING OF THE END: APEX
THOSE IN POWER MAGNIFY IDEAS
CHRISTIANS ARE HATED FOR LINES
NARCISSISTS CAN'T SELF-CORRECT
I HATE THE PHONE/EMAIL ONLY
COVER HER SINS NOT GOSSIP ABOUT EM
KINGS AND SULTANS FALL/ARE KILLED
TO BE GREAT
THEY SENSED I WAS SMARTER
BETRAYAL-TRAUMATIZATION
100% APPROVAL BY EVERYONE
PTSD AND UNHAPPY MEMORIES
DUNNING-KRUGER LOSERS
AVOID CREEPY AND DARK
THIS IS SATAN, DON'T LET HIM

EVIL FREAKS

EVIL FREAKS

EVIL FREAKS HUMILIATE

The evil freaks are so insecure it's a compensatory mechanism to humiliate others.

Tho' plentiful they are freaks of nature since humans should support and help each other.

From their position of self-hate bringing you down to compensate is all they think about mate.

It's not so much they hate you as conservative but that you are independent [drumbeat different].

If you take that s**t they're gonna continue to dish it, that's just the nature of the narcissist.

A queen only dates men to get information not to have sex with them. Get some class vixens.

LIBERALS CODDLE CRIMINALS

Every animal has means to defend itself--and will--but the liberal female even coddles criminals.

Because our female emotions are as deep as the ocean no man can know them so watch em.

Any queen who's experienced that will never experience that again, it's too demeaning.

The ten thousand women you had were common, see that you haunted house of demons.

It was like a machine. They thought they owned me and I didn't have boundaries see.

If from a trauma background you feel shame, so when anyone blinks you respond with the same.

TRIGGERED SHAME

Even a child becomes an authority figure triggering shame with one who's primed early ok.

See shame wash over a child like this and it doesn't take much for him to fall into the ditch.

It's a limbic response of the child when they feel a disconnect with mom: a trauma bond.

Children are egocentric--it's all their fault they think--so do anything to get back into sync.

The traumatized rarely grow out of a childlike response to disapproval, easily becoming tools.

The traumatized freeze like a child when violated but without the life skills going against it.

FREEZING WITH INVASION

The default to push someone away is established as children or they freeze up with dismay.

When coming from dysfunctional homes life skills were never learned: we must play catch up.

Sticking up for oneself means being an adult. It begins with finding self, diamond in the rough.

It's common not to stick up for self when a boundary's been crossed but it shows the boss.

Who knew I shoulda learned self-defense before going off the college? I didn't/it was a mess.

It was my job to do this or that, they owned me--just cuz I didn't have a me, an open sea.

What I needed was totally irrelevant and expressing a need was seen as selfish to them.

Many parents were immature children in adult bodies. That's where it all starts: total insanity.

Tho' a recovered adult child of alcoholics there are still consequences raised by lunatics.

The emotionally arrested children act like children when bringing up their children, amen.

It's not your fault if intentionally raised to be just as dysfunctional as your forebearers.

I'm not saying it happened to me or you but isn't it logical with the imprint of early trauma?

The pattern doesn't just continue it expands cuz life is holographic and nothing stays the same.

KNOW/OWN YOUR FEELINGS

To defend the self one must KNOW his feelings but the un-self aware can't say "knock it off now".

The child feels powerless being dependent on the bigger/stronger but he can't identify it.

Center yourself, know how you feel: now you're ready to stick up for yourself and be truly real.

If you don't even know your feelings or values how can you set boundaries? It's like A, B then C.

EVIL FREAKS

Without a sense of self you won't know a boundary's been crossed you'll just be pissed off.

Tho' filled with humiliation at what just happened a busted boundary she never mentioned.

STAND UP FOR YOURSELF

She froze at his inconsideration/was filled with disgust but never mentioned a line was crossed.

He has audacity to say cruel things then act like it's a joke: what it's like being unequally yoked.

Utterly deceiving: Since a narcissist has no self he has a million selves and keeps changing.

In order to stick up for yourself you must see what'll happen if you don't. Have foresight, duh!

If you don't stand up for yourself they will walk all over you & try to kill you when you finally do.

Instead of being overwhelmed by a limbic brain panic response, try standing up for yourself.

She just wants to end the pain now, not think of what will happen is she doesn't say "NO!"

Upset someone doesn't like us, triggered guilt and shame, overwhelmed as they invade.

In order to set a boundary, see into the future to know what will happen if you don't and hurry.

Biden's Foreign Policy: Speak softy and carry no stick, just be part of the club. Bill Bennett

We're going down so fast, a sinking ship. Where's Trump, are arrests made as promised?

IMPOSING INGRATES

Oh you who've had ten thousand women: you're a haunted house of a million demons.

When you push back/stick up for yourself get ready for the consequences/reactions from hell.

The narcissistic boy kept busting my boundaries, a refusal to beckon to any authority.

The narcissist wanted me, money, food/water, time/energy and to use my washing machine.

Joyce Meyers doesn't brood over being raped 200 times by age ten. She's gone ahead.

Don't let him bring his laundry over--send him to the laundromat. It's little things like that.

Jezebel is a borrower and never returner, an officious busybody and traitor who strikes terror.

Jezebel brings her friends who's she's already primed against you as she plays innocent shrew.

BOUNDARIES HAVE CONSEQUENCES

It's immature not to have foresight. If you gossip about a friend imagine the reaction tonight.

It's facing consequences of outcomes we can't control: a loose canon cuz we didn't see the whole.

Codependents are notorious for talking themselves outa their intuition--heed your gut son.

A narc's victim is gaslit and trauma bonded to the point she no longer trusts her instincts ok.

EVIL FREAKS

I'm a high wall now but there was a time I laid right down and let em walk over my lines.

I was so horrified by my circumstances I went cold to all of it and just accepted the dam rats.

A Jezebel walks so crooked she can't be trusted: the chaos she creates has consequences.

Honoring how you feel is keeping your boundaries despite any possible consequences.

THEY LIKE THE AGREABLE

They liked me when I was so agreeable but the minute I stuck up for myself they had a cow.

You're easy to tolerate/be around if you're not gonna confront them, just a get along.

If a clingy person who wants you to be everything for them is pushed back, they won't like it.

If they bust your boundaries again you can't back down. You must further up/tell the town.

The wicked man CREEPS into women's houses, those laden with sins so they accept the louses.

He creeps one step at a time taking over homes but this never happens to Queens, oh no.

You won't crumble when the consequence is rejection, this is all faced by a mature person.

Must help your brain to be liberated, since fear prevents setting boundaries/being protected.

The minute you back down/clam up after setting a boundary, oh man get ready for tragedy.

My big fear was her smear campaign the minute I drew a line, or violence from her allies.

To her, drawing a line was being mean. If they can't have a piece they destroy your scene.

With fear of consequences from setting boundaries the limbic brain is activated: we clam up.

She thinks: "It's MY fault I'm upset". And they agree--she's just a bitch and a martinet.

BOUNDARY BLOCKERS

It's hard to set a boundary if you're programmed to think it's your fault, always being sorry.

Think about the possible rejection and learn to be ok with that. Now draw the line, and wait.

To set boundaries without fear of abandonment brings spiritual joy, freedom and ELATION.

It means you've pulled back from codependency and seeking the outer world's validation see.

The journey outa codependency is a SPIRITUAL one as you see how dysfunctional it was hon'.

Whether it's social media with likes & fans or a narc relationship reeling you in, it's trauma man.

It's disgusting when you're people pleasing to regain the narc's approval after rug removal.

In a universe of evolving beings you'll experience nirvana without these attachments.

Learning to be comfortable with disagreements is a very adult move. Be firm I behoove.

It's the nature of humans to form attachments. Here's the downside for your protection plans.

When grifters raid you at midnight you can't stay passive aggressive, gotta push back.

Stick up for self or stuff it, drink it, snort it. Frustration leads to aggression and addicts.

So now when they bring 100 people to your thanksgiving blast you'll know to push back.

BOUNDARIES AND RED FLAGS

Set a. boundary against this incident or a precedent is set getting worse for the next event.

You told him to invite whoever he wanted so he brought fifty people. What will you do shrew?

Women see sex giving them power but there's never been a female generation less empowered.

Hopefulness makes us ignore red flags. Like hot and cold players and dream hooks of cads.

Trauma blinds us to red flags so pay attention to LITTLE FEELINGS normally dismissed.

I'm so sorry but if you've had that many women you're filled with demons so kindly move on.

What you call "dating" is just fornication. Dating is to get information not have sex with em.

BEST FRIENDS AND HUSBANDS

The narcissist operates in alternate reality: a false front/story propped up as a cover up.

Most women don't have a "best friend" or her B.F. is on the phone next revealing all to her ex.

Most men know that she doesn't have a best friend, because hell they've slept with them.

With the loyalty of rattlesnakes their jealousy of each other make women natural traitors ok.

The betrayals of women/feminized men are insidious and cancerous cuz they talk too much.

You've got a friend in Jesus but after that know anyone's capable of stabbing your back.

Women "friends" love to get with your husband and spill the beans and it's you they demean.

They're jealous your husband favors you over them, not understanding marriage in sum.

Don't get such a big house that you need a maid. They've got big ears and repeat everything ok?

They used to go about their work silently so life went on, now they cause trouble in the home.

WOMEN DON'T HAVE BEST FRIENDS

Tho' I was paying her she rose up against me constantly doing things her own way: contumacy.

"I didn't like her coming over with him here and eventually I found they slept together". Wife

Men have slept with her, her mother, her sisters, her best friend, whoever she's been around.

They're dogs who have sex with whoever they've been around but a good wife cuts these bands.

EVIL FREAKS

The point is: don't tell anyone your plans. NO ONE. Tell only God and sure victory will come.

In any plan to escape or enter a relationship you need prayer and supplication not gossipin'.

Whatever it is you do you do so well, it's a unique art form you've developed that rings a bell.

Don't think back to when you were one-down in that system, it's an anchor to mockery/derision.

Stop playing a losing game. Walk away from the table cuz it's rigged and you gotta stop playing.

To fully recover you must be removed from the game much like any athlete racked with pain.

SEPARATE YE

Separate yourself from the source of your poisoning--go no contact--and that starts healing.

"Get out from amongst them and I will receive you": the separation brings instant bliss too.

Isolation from toxicity brings emo-psycho insulation of the soul: there's no more impact now.

The problem is being gamed & released into a toxic world with no insulation, remember girl?

Increments of increased separation: from frenemies, family and society's narratives around me.

Adaptation to dyads & triads in human systems is hell when so un-self aware, an empty shell.

Embrace the pain of withdrawal cuz it's gonna hurt but the future's bright after removing a curse.

EVIL FREAKS

Like a heroine addict you may long for your abuser if only to get even but both are bummers.

It was so awful living in the orbit of others when blind to the game which can't be won, ever.

When I escaped him [a dark den] my world opened up like a bright light surrounded by friends.

My persecutors all died or blew away like the chaff, too irrelevant & pathetic to try to get back.

Those who fired me or lent an ear to gossipers were all gone, I looked for them and saw nothing.

TWO STATES: GRATING OR HUMMING

It was all a reflection of where I was at: If in sin my world turned dim, a dangerous den.

If repentant my world turned bright and creative working all day optimistic and joyous.

I was either humming or grating with the universe and who I associate with was the main curse.

They ignore your achievements & bring up your sinful past. Bid these frenemies good riddance.

Associate with this person, a grey cloud. Dis-associate and you're back into the happy fold.

As I look back God was always Champion and Protector, enemies are gone or down under.

GOD TOOK EM ALL OUT

Instead of looking back with resentment or remorse, think of your foe's outcome: he's toast.

EVIL FREAKS

They scared me so much I feared for my life then suddenly they were gone, no more strife.

As a naive sheltered girl I put myself at his mercy but God gave me escape anyway, hurray.

A dumb guy had total control of me cuz I naively put myself at his mercy, but for Big Daddy.

I shudder looking back at my thin escapes but God always shows at the last minute mate.

ESCAPE THE GROSS GUY

Escape the gross guy too: though he's popular with the devil's crowd he'll be your Waterloo.

An old man making adolescent remarks about sex: stay away from such for his ugly evil's complex.

An old woman making remarks about sex: this is even uglier because from us more is expected.

The unfairness of it all: the rat race, the status climb, favoritism, comparisons all the time.

The innate hatred of evil world towards goodness [which it calls badness] and mental illness.

To be gamed is a losing game so all you can do is forgive them and move on, educated.

My whole life was a series of increasing disentanglements and feeling relieved joy again.

It's gonna hurt as you shift levels from being a queen controlled by a clown or the devil.

Embrace the pain to escape the bondage. Break your heart so your soul will heal, finally.

EVIL FREAKS

The pain is pregnant with possibilities so don't avoid it, get into it along with self-improvement see.

SHAME FOR OLD ASSOCIATIONS

Shame and guilt are some of the pains of withdrawal along with wanting more synthetic love.

I was ashamed I allowed such a shallow fellow depleted of character--so low--to have all control.

Inferior in character, intellectually and spiritually--and yet the queen hands it over: her sanity.

There are jewels in your pain/shame and they're called lessons. Pain is the megaphone of wisdom.

If you embrace the pain looking for the lessons you find all you need to know just experiencing them.

Don't miss the teacher in the pain by being so busy getting rid of it: you gotta feel it man.

You gotta feel it to heal it, embrace it to see the pearls through it: take it from me I overcame it.

I went thru it and was done with it, a wise woman. There are those who obsess but no wisdom.

Now you unlearn & relearn: what femininity is, what a relationship should look like, false concerns.

Girlie you don't stir a man up sexually and then expect him to see your heart or intellectually.

THE UNAPPRECIATED GOOD HUSBAND

You brought the sex in out of turn so now you must reject false metrics of value, of YOU.

EVIL FREAKS

A broken woman jumps like a circus animal to the call of an abusive man who is noncommittal.

But then she can't submit to a good husband who loves, respects, cares and supports her?

Live on the streets for awhile to appreciate a good husband who loves/supports you shrew.

A good husband who keeps her head above water and brings stability to her home is "boring"?

Adapt to a narcissist for awhile and you'll appreciate a good husband who keeps you in style.

Call an old "friend" to hear him bring your sins up again then you'll appreciate a forgiving husband.

Live with a meanie who drops you off in other cities then appreciate a husband with morality.

Live with a mean cad [every day's a black cloud] now appreciate your husband's stable moods.

Live around a gross pig always talking about sex now appreciate your husband's sweetness.

IT'S HARD TO FORGET IT ALL

The only thing about cutting off the past is you sit in it for awhile but these war stories won't last.

Once finally in freedom behind a locked gate you sit tortured by thoughts of the old days.

What makes a strong independent woman compliant to the toxic demands of an abusive man?

The abusive man injects language into her soul that like a script reinforces her own bondage.

25

EVIL FREAKS

The way he sees/acts towards her acts as a program for her "unexplained" crazy behavior.

If he doesn't treat you right he doesn't teach you right as the toxic male ALWAYS backbites.

You will never please toxic male culture--the oppressor will never empower-- the OPPRESSED.

You can do everything on his list but nothing's ever good enough, gotta keep hopping.

A season just for you--in self-discovery, self-definition, self-development-- before relationship.

Before you see the world thru healthy eyes you will always ascribe value to trash, aye.

Ascribing value to trash in discernment of assets: I'd say this describes me in the past.

To know thyself, look at your history and what you've gone through. I do that all day long too.

Why you hear what you do, why you accept what you shouldn't: self-therapy in browsing back.

SELF-DISCOVERY

It's not a narcissistic trip to explore self-discovery & self-development as destiny's equipped.

Put energy into what you like, what makes you happy, how you help the world, NOT THAT GUY.

When you don't know who you are you accept it ALL because you have no boundaries doll.

How she recovers from the game: by learning how to appreciate Actual Value not this shame.

EVIL FREAKS

Appreciate your actual value and the clown's too. Marry your purpose: that's what you DO.

I am enough as I am, I don't perform for anybody, I'm only pressured by my own striving see.

Be not angry intentionally cuz God'll bring you into new circles and people treating you nicely.

In your Season of Selfishness you discover who you are, a formal introduction to a star.

My sister tyrant "trustee" paid the bills while she spilled the beans, laying evil seeds.

Prince Charming loves Cinderella for who she is as she finally escapes her sisters/those fellas.

FEMINIST BACKLASH

Men traditionally protect women but now they're being drained of self-confidence/broken down.

The backlash femme: the consciousness of women *intentionally* broken down by men.

The trauma-bonded woman doesn't have a clue to the trap she's in when later systems sting.

Dad just told me to hold my head up high, not the specific battles I'd have day and night.

I felt hated right away, I'd have to defend myself from strangers ok and life was hell this way.

Once whipped by one system you're a bull's eye in the next and that's how it spreads out, hexed.

Living in a life of hatred due to evil seeds planted by false brethren was my calumnious end.

DON'T HEX NEW SYSTEMS

Don't hex new systems by crying about the old ones but write of psych persecution to the end.

Write about the subtle interactional devices that are killing by inciting riots or institutionalizing.

Write about how sisters ruin sisters and even mothers hate their own daughters. I still shudder.

Once you see it as a system working like a machine you can self-actualize by releasing the fiends.

They kept the smartest/most likely to succeed daughter down in the dumps as a chump.

And because they were older/the majority everyone believed them and the victim caved in.

Because the matrix was always two against one, the victim accepted grasshopper status then.

In her daily diary she wrote "triangulation is strangulation" because it was hell man.

Many women taking men seriously while men are playing games: broken hearts from the start.

How does a man take a woman and break her down to where she's about to lose her mind?

She's so embattled she accepts any abuse and even when he flatly rejects her she pursues.

Why does he rattle her cage over & over again? Well, it's intentional which she sees at the end.

He penetrates her defenses by being her dream man but her knight in shining armor is an actor.

Thru calculated conversation he breaks her down to having a sexual relationship with him.

PHASE TWO: HOOK HER ON HIM

Phase Two: The man becomes the woman's emotional addiction to fix an early trauma of rejection.

The early abandonment was so great all her energy went to the addictive devices of escape.

He wants her strung out on a drug: he's her emotional addiction ever bashing her like a thug.

He consumes all her time, flatters her/tells her what she wants to hear then becomes a pervert.

He'll push her to level 3, she agrees. Then he pushes her to four, five, six until she's crazy.

Like a moth to the flame the more he pushes her limits the more addicted she becomes to him.

The more she gives herself to him the less she possesses of self anymore: low attraction.

He's deceived her with calculated conversation, creates a soul tie then he avoids commitment.

When foolish I was dealing with those more foolish than I and what a total disaster, aye.

TOXIC MASCULINITY

For a toxic narcissistic man to exist in his world requires the subjugation of women.

Her dream not reality: If I give him this/that and become this/that to him he'll marry me finally.

Even if he marries to gain financially he won't stay true in a generation of toxic masculinity.

Toxic masculinity is violent but that she sees as protective even if sexually aggressive.

A generation of women with broken consciousness are made to believe these are attractive.

Toxic Men are: lovers of self, lovers of pleasure more than God, traitors, highminded deceivers.

Toxic masculinity feeds on the marginalizations of women so at every turn you're feeling em.

A QUEEN ASLEEP

Broken consciousness is a queen asleep. She cannot rule or reign, an empty shell, not a peep.

Women today are sleeping queens. All of the power in the kingdom but to men's devices, asleep.

He breaks her consciousness and then she participates in her own humiliation/dishonor.

A drug addicts knows inside every time he goes back he brings on his own dishonor, aye.

Addiction defined for free: I don't need this, this is killing me, but give it to me quickly.

A woman is conditioned to be attracted to emotionally unavailable men seeking to break her.

She doesn't want a good man, just an emotionally unavailable one breaking her down.

It's not your imagination that he's breaking you down by bringing up your past with a frown.

EVIL FREAKS

Men seeking to break em: women being managed by inferiors not having their best interest sir.

Women have grasshopper status without a man so are conditioned to settle for an inferior one.

You let em in to charge their phone and they'll gossip to all and take over your whole home.

If her dissembling weren't so infuriating it'd be hilarious but see the tragic consequences, you must.

TOXIC MASCULINITY ADDICTS

Maturity is going from men who tear her down to a man who worships the ground she walks on.

Toxic masculinity is low self-esteem compensating by bringing a woman down and it's planned.

It's a compensatory unconscious mechanism to keep the ego above water/from drowning.

A queen going to a lesser man thinking he'll stay in is put thru the ringer with compensations.

HIGH VALUE MEN WITH LOW PROFILES

From high profile but immature men to a high value man, a godly man & humble/no fans.

The cost of freedom is the same with a person: You must overcome, dissociate and go on.

Stop ruminating over the lesson. You'll never have to go thru it again cuz you've overcome him.

Narcissist is an actor covering emptiness inside. With problems he just reinvents himself, aye.

She hates toxic masculinity while being addicted to it but when she finally sees she rejects it.

Signs you have grown: Just as you overcame alcohol it's the same with people pulling you down.

Just as you overcame odd girl out status and caving into the mess you will overcome this.

Once safely behind a locked gate I collected all the hate denied for years in order to be great.

They will love you if you're part of their own but if you're different they'll deride, mock, shun.

"I'M THE ONE YOU'RE WAITING FOR"

Broken consciousness degrades attractions until you're so bitter you literally hate all men.

You're surrounded by men who'd make great husbands and kings but you say "nothing here".

They creep into houses leading silly women laden with sins and diverse lusts [food, alcohol, sex].

Digging deeper in his profile: You'll find your knight in shining armor is mere aluminum foil.

He already knows you're conditioned to want/need a man so slides right in saying "I'm the one".

"I'm the one you're waiting for" as he wants husband rights without any commitment declared.

Purity: No you can't come in I wanna be alone. Sins: Come right in and take over my home.

He slides in as your DREAM taking care of everything then withholds your desire, a wedding.

EVIL FREAKS

WITHHOLDING DESIRE TO BREAK YOU

"He purposely withholds desire to break you" said therapist to a shrew who's psychotic too.

You date [ascertain desire to commit], you marry, you have sex. That's the order that's best.

Having sex in the dating period is a losing game as one takes the reins and the other degrades.

The more he withholds the emptier you become and the more control he has of your soul.

There's no reason to date a man who won't commit to marriage. It's a waste of time, a mirage.

When you give a man more than you should you operate from shame and a heart of wood.

YOU GAVE TOO DAM MUCH

You gave him more than you're comfortable with and now you're emotionally down in a ditch.

You gave him more than what you felt was right and now he's backing out like after a fight.

Stupid girl, that was all the leverage you had. A queen with self-esteem would never do that!

Hope deferred makes the heart sick. The more he builds up & withholds the sicker she gets.

It's his intent as she gets further down. He's had to traumatize her to deflate her crown.

Traumatize to deflate her crown = MANAGE her without any trouble holding her down.

Path that stinks: You're just part of the team you think as he withholds your desire for exclusivity.

NO HUSBAND BENEFITS!

He doesn't even have the qualities to commit yet you're giving him **HUSBAND** benefits?

End run: He's caught with other women and you forgive him & he does it again and again.

THIS is what you get when you hold onto a dream which is really a nightmare, amen.

Girl you're gonna have to endure some pain by breaking the soul tie and ejecting that guy.

Count your losses, learn and regather yourself--or face the PAIN of wasted life with nothing left.

I've laid it out for you dames. Choose your pain but never say no one told you about the game.

Some men attract women but that's not you hon'. A lady never chases men, she waits for the ONE.

ROOT CAUSES AD NAUSEUM

Their search for "root causes" means they have no intention of solving the problem.

I know what it's like when God removes the hedge of protection, when unvetted evil flows in.

The looney leftists blame police for out of control crime in all blue cities not themselves.

The problem with Critical Race Theory is if you say you're not a racist that means you are.

MORE LOVE MORE DEVASTATION

They loved SO much the deception took em out or disordered their brain & nervous system.

I was leery of everyone, I had to control everything, I was jealous, anxious, muted, distraught.

Emotional baggage is hell coming thru to ruin the present moment. It discolors all of it.

Emotional baggage plus shame is too much to take but toxic shame is inherited & part of the game.

You're not aware of how you're sabotaging new relationships until you understand baggage.

It's a jungle mentality of always shooting at shadows and looking for ways out [being a nut].

You trusted way too early before trustworthy and got hurt again pulling back to your den.

All my internal circuitry of free-flowing spontaneous creativity was blocked by this blow see.

When creativity is lost & synaptic clarity is blocked one looks opaque not translucent/glossed.

VICTIMS MAKE POOR FRIENDS

The victim tends to treat people poorly cuz they don't trust em thus bringing more opprobrium.

For fulfilling relationships deal with your emotional baggage because that's what ruins them.

Above all don't add insult to injury by shaming yourself for being abused. That's obvious.

Don't layer shame on top of an emotional wound. Remove shame, heal wound and go on.

That's what it means to "unpack": Remove layers of shame on top of trauma then face facts.

If you're needy or in need of approval that's an opportunity to unpack it for removal.

Recognize your trauma triggers but don't expect the new person to adapt, work on em first.

Betrayal and abandonment trauma are important concepts to understand when unraveling.

You don't know the heart of a person until they know your secrets. Shut your mouth/be smart.

DISCIPLINE MAKES KINGS

It's not power that makes kings, it's discipline. Keep your mouth from approval-getting son.

Discipline expands your borders and increases your capacity whereas power not necessarily.

Samson had the power of a king but he lacked the discipline see so died a slave, blinded.

He opened his mouth to someone he could not trust, Delilah. Who are you blabbing to sista?

A king doesn't yak to get approval or brag about how much he makes. These give him away.

If a person runs their mouth too much on their business you must never tell them yours.

Make your plans and execute in silence. Never tell them until afterwards with sure success.

By the time the foe knows what's up the work is already in progress and can't be stopped.

EVIL FREAKS

Let your war be waged in silence and let your victory speak for itself in Kingly nonchalance.

A main reason for kingly nonchalance is success changes attitudes around you fast.

Never celebrate victories with enemies cuz in fear they hate you more for these dreams.

They already hate you for jealousy/envy are the biggest human emotions and you're royalty.

Your winning is not gonna make em like you or love you but if you let em they'll try to use you.

Just cuz they're related to you doesn't mean they're happy with your success, get a clue.

Find the people who've been proven in your world and celebrate with them finding the pearl.

What, I brought so much opprobrium onto myself in order to learn and write books? Unreal.

COMING OUT OF DENIAL

The older I get the more I see what they did, a safety mechanism back then to stay above it.

I'm too much of a prude for your circle. Say stuff like that to insulate yourself from people.

You're royalty speaking from a podium uninterrupted by the rabble, not part of a roundtable.

I never spoke of my plans or what I was doing for all those years--decades working/waiting.

EVIL FREAKS

If interviewer has an obvious dirty mind and objectifies women why would you ever do it?

I only have one life to express myself bud, not gonna let you hold me down in the mud.

About going out there I'm delirious. I may even have to hire a therapist it's so serious.

I got one word for women replacing all other words to y'all: He Don't Want You Or You'd Know.

There's a war on women you can't tell me there's not. Flip-flops, insults, accusations, shit-shots.

It must be a backlash against feminism cuz in patriarchy they were treated with respect.

There's a war on women and a queen knows it. She's prepared, is chaperoned and wins it.

I felt like a pin cushion always running back to my husband for solace after accusation.

I went into monastic isolation and felt so happy for the first time. No one ever sees me, aye.

THEY BRING EVIL GOSSIP

They'd bring me evil gossip by people I didn't know. Somehow there's always an undertow.

There's a war on women like they have a bull's eye painted on em: marriage is protection.

A female genius must be married in an orderly home behind a locked gate: good fate.

By the time she finally reaches success she's utterly exhausted after fighting this mess.

EVIL FREAKS

Find one who loves you and forget the rest. Use this method until popularity is blessed.

Stay within your own circle and remember: everyone's on probation with you-- no bummers.

The female genius has no women friends and she can't trust many men especially when young.

A female genius either lands on Lord & Jesus as Friend & Champion or it's a rough end.

They just wanna find new ways to sell out men's rights to a fair hearing for woke approval getting.

It's the accused who's lost his liberties as his home is raided, guns taken and rep degraded.

EVIL FREAKS

It's the hardest thing in life to face a mad crowd sided against you triggered by a cad you knew.

The gut-pain in solar plexus from being screwed royally by those closet cannot be expressed.

Don't worry, people always show their immaturities unknowingly cuz they don't study me.

Recognize these social devices keeping You down cuz it's always by clowns wearing crowns.

I was always sided against: the dumbed mob and the inconvenient woman with thoughts.

I was born in hot water. But that's also the case under King Herod with the birth of the savior.

I was different from the beginning and could NOT adapt to social devices and silly grinning.

They hated the odd girl out in every social arena and I always ended up escaping/crying for momma.

EXPERT SOCIAL MANIPULATORS

So it was easy for Jolly Jimmy to socially victimize me when his guilt for drinking needed covering.

Keep a thought central: We all have a right to self-respect, decency, civility and this ain't it see.

We have to heal from all this in order to not poison the future through disrespecting new links.

40

EVIL FREAKS

It's all about character: when he's put you down like a wrestler it's crucial you know who you are.

Jolly Jimmy was an expert social manipulator despite being a drinker so I was seen as the stinker.

I took him in to prop me up [the queen] but when he changed I degraded: it's like a machine.

All behavior is compensatory when ruled by jealousy a sign of low minds anyway who can't see.

She was so jealous of me she HAD to get her flying monkeys against me/hit men treachery.

She was so jealous of me she HAD to even things up any way she could even with criminality.

She "loved" her daughter but was so jealous she HAD to sabotage her plans even her destiny.

NARCISSISTS USE PUBLIC HUMILIATION

Watch how a narcissist undercuts your authority: whether business or social it's treachery.

Humiliation reveals their brokenness but knowing that doesn't help when caught in this chaos.

Humiliation is meant to create trauma. Narcissists know what they're doing, way beyond drama.

Keeping you traumatized keeps them totally in control in your situation. Honey, please escape him!

Witnesses to your humiliation buy into the narc's propaganda: you're ostracized in that system.

Witnesses don't see context/you can't talk it out with em so they slide in with the condemnation.

They didn't understand me to begin with so his humiliation of me brought their surety.

With years in the system I'd ask "is there anyone who gets me?" I was totally alone & unfree.

It's the most insidious thing they do: build themselves up at someone else's expense, whew.

He's jolly Jimmy when he drinks but how he treats his wife stinks so they see her as the fink.

No one can make you feel inferior without your consent but as a social scapegoat you're dead.

You've grown, you don't have a need to humiliate others. See this about your character.

The true mark of good character is overcoming: getting back up, learning and growing.

What good is it to go thru all this without giving you the benefit of my life lessons with twits?

The way out: Anchor down on your good character with self-respect and civility towards yourself.

The idea of helping and supporting each other thru trials & success is lost to the narcissist.

Feeling civility towards yourself is a gift that no narcissist can take away from you.

THE KING

A great man, a king, is governed by his integrity whereas a lesser man seeks notoriety.

If she's an evil freak when she drinks he'll drop her quick because it reflects on him, a king.

EVIL FREAKS

A great man's image reflects his character, a lesser man not, he is two and one's a tiger.

Who can find a virtuous woman, who can find a faithful man? It's better to be alone until then.

There's not enough depth in a common man or woman to recognize character like I'm describin'

Most women are not accustomed to dealing with kings since the world is full of clowns, ya think?

THE PIMP

A PIMP struggles with his low self-esteem by playing psych games on women till they scream.

An underachiever, the manipulation of woman gives him a sick sense of manhood over her.

To manage females to his advantage gives him a false sense of manhood despite any damage.

He learns at the barbershop to be a man he must manage, manipulate and control nonstop.

He learns about the average women: to gain control you must emotionally abuse them.

Abuse triggers her early trauma when rejected by momma inciting her love for this monster.

The underachieving pimp feels he can only achieve manhood by controlling a woman.

Gaining power thru emotional abuse: leaving you off in other cities and even killing your pet too.

The underachieving pimp is gonna pull the queen down, it's a no-brainer compulsion.

EVIL FREAKS

Pimp has gotta be mean, that's the recipe to make himself a man again. Don't trust he'll change.

He's gotta get her in tears so in her collapsed state his low self-esteem repairs/he's kicked upstairs.

Men compelled to be mean to women: It's happening FAR more today than before feminism.

FRANTIC WOMEN ON THE CHASE

A woman gets so weak she gets frantic and chases men and is rejected again by a lowmind.

That's the system: Queen hankers for lowminds beneath her so she too becomes a commoner.

She defers to a commoner thinking he's far more likely to stay with her and only goes under.

PIMPDOM: To be a man I need to manage, manipulate, control and emotionally abuse women.

In the last days perilous times shall come. Men loving themselves and covetous. 2 Timothy 3: 1-6

They are fierce and despise those who are good. Traitors, heady, lovers of pleasure not God.

Without natural affection, truce breakers, false accusers, deceptive social manipulators.

Enemies are covetous, boasters, proud blasphemers, disobedient to parents, unthankful, unholy.

They have a form of godliness but it's powerless. They lead captive silly women in their houses.

A pimp *creeps* into houses to control women laden with sins and led away by diverse lusts.

EVIL FREAKS

These guys are so self-consumed they find the most gullible woman and lead her to ruin.

SIMPS AND SINFUL WOMEN

A **SIMP** moves into her house as another child. He has no self-respect but enjoys the good life.

A silly woman laden with sins wants his company due to sin's consequence: lower companions.

To earn his cushy existence he props her up and she desperately depends on that non-stop.

He says "I'm just gonna let her have her way/do what she wants to do, say yes to everything".

As he turns yes-man she takes a nose dive confirmed all the way until he rejects the savage finally.

A real man brings **ORDER** to the household not simp-like yes-man approval with hell to pay.

It's as bad as girlfriends giving approval for sins such as affairs, driving her down to the gutter.

One feminist frenemy encouraged her to sleep with her student, driving her into firing and ruin.

There's gonna be a severe undertow hanging with underachievers due to this natural matrix.

It's not the will of God for a man to be a tyrant or the opposite, jumping to her will like a twit.

Eventually she decides she does not want a pimp nor a simp: losers bringing down the ship.

The **LEADER** in the house should not be given to wine, no striker or brawler but patient with wife.

He's not selfish and self-centered but ruling his house having his children under subjection.

A KING LEADS FAMILY AND GOV

If a man can't lead his own woman, how can he lead the church or his own governments?

A "king" knows who he is/where he's going. He has depth, knowing his role and his wife's always.

A king doesn't have a problem with saying "honey, why don't you take the lead on that?"

He never demands submission, he honors his woman so well that submission is natural, amen.

Some women want a pimp. Their traumatized/broken consciousness makes em moved by it.

Many women want a simp: may have a little paycheck but still just another child at the house.

I'm talking to women who want a king. There are five things designating him in the main.

1. A king wants a woman who is his exclusively and EXCLUSIVITY rules his whole life see.

A man wants a virtuous woman--not meaning virginal. She manages her good reputation that's all.

To be too available turns him off, a king isn't interested in a woman who's running him down.

He thinks: If she's pursuing me like this she could be two others. A desperate woman bothers.

A desperate woman won't get noticed by a king cuz he can't trust her ability to be exclusive.

Kings/queens will never share. Once it's exposed they'll dust their hands/open to future.

Because exclusivity is most important to a king, he's not checking her phone just trusting.

The heart of her husband doth safely trust in her: that's talking about the virtuous woman sir.

A KING MUST *SAFELY* TRUST HER

A king needs to *safely* trust in her, so that she can do him good all the days of her life.

A king must trust her with his money, name and reputation--for this he seeks a virtuous woman.

There's a way his wife carries herself: very polite, not high/mighty but with high boundaries.

The virtuous wife weaves thru the whole room while still showing she's completely exclusive.

He's checking her out: her accessibility to certain types or does she social climb/name drop?

He wants one happy and fulfilled in herself but with a style saying "I'm open to the right situation".

It is Marxist due process: "There's no proof that he DIDN'T plan [Trump's] insurrection"

THE KING'S ATTRACTIONS

A king values one who represents herself well. She makes the load lighter/the road brighter.

If her presentation is phenomenal the king thinks "here is a woman who will represent ME well".

A king of a man wants a woman who inspires him and represents him better than he himself.

A king waits for a woman who draws the line. Even in a bad time he'll respect how she refines.

If she objects to his language he'll happily pull back cuz he got he wanted, a woman with spine.

She moves thru the room of people with grace but her boundaries are evident, keep your space.

Listening to music looking out the window in delightful reverie and add some cannabis for me.

A king is looking for a woman who draws the line cuz kings have firm boundaries at all times.

A king wants from a woman what he's willing to give to a woman and that's loyalty to the end.

The quality of a man's woman can rescue that man from calamity in life's bad seasons see.

She must have the temperament/intellectual or visionary capacity to form a power couple.

TWO KINGDOMS MERGING

It's the merger of two huge kingdoms, so the real man doesn't want to Lord it over his woman.

Nor is he willing to slide in and use her--take advantage of her accomplishments ever.

A king looks for one he can build with. But when she asks questions pimps/simps get nervous.

Kings love questions [revealing the depth of her consciousness] but pimps/simps hate em.

He wants a high-value partnership so loves her questions triggering his conceptions.

It's the ying and yang. It's the way things work together with the male vs. female brain.

TRUE KINGS LOVE DEEP QUESTIONS

Kings appreciate deep complex questions and kings can answer them, that's the attraction.

Deep questions indicate the potential he has with her to create a high-value partnership.

Who is he who can find an excellent woman [spiritual, capable, intelligent and virtuous]?

Kings are looking not for dependents but independent women who run their own kingdoms.

A king is looking for one who helps his life to multiply, encouraging her business on the side.

In a high value partnership it's heirs together of the grace of life. He honors her/she submits, aye.

Then they create something together that they never could have separately. 2 + 2 = Infinity.

The last point about a great man: If you respect him you can have anything, that's his plan.

To get a king the great woman must heal from the impact of previous experiences with men.

The traumas caused by inferior men are worn on the face, in the posture, in everything she says.

You wear trauma in your energy, it comes out in your tone and just about everybody knows.

EVIL FREAKS

In many cases one disrespects respectable people due to projections from previous bad aspects.

The unhealed pain of the past poisons present opportunities as it disrespects new links.

Wives submit yourselves for the man is the head. Respect your husband and he will cherish you.

THE DEFAULT IS EVIL FREAKS

Listen to a teaching video then look out the window. Ruminate, absorb it and then you know.

Success comes with being comfortable with uncertainty and taking risks. Geo Bruno

I have a right to be hoity toity I did the work Missy not just selfies in self glory without booty.

No worries: Even tho' you were a raving madwoman they still saw the genius of the situation.

Stop talking about your age ["at my age", I'm gonna be 61"] for it's just an identity and anti-sage.

The audacious boldness comes in words but if you were to meet me I'm gentle as a little bird.

I love cats, dogs and seasons of the day. Social gatherings bore me and I wanna escape.

I thank God for the great and marvelous work He gave me to do & I pray you gain from it too.

It seemed apropos but now remorse. Don't worry, they always saw the genius of the situation.

Biden loves being popular in the world fake club, one of those globalist guys all dressed up.

EVIL FREAKS

NARCISSISTIC INJURY

"I'm waiting for you to complete me" said a Queen to a creep cuz a trauma bond confused her see.

If you lay a boundary or say NO while staying bold it constitutes narcissistic injury to this foe.

Saying NO to the narcissist creates emotional injury since he's the center of the universe you see.

When you say NO and mean it get ready for their EXIT [unless they need you in the hiatus], forget it.

When the one begins to show strength of any kind the narcissist plans his exit strategy/realigns.

In the mind of the narcissist you can't have any stature. He thinks: if you're strong he's weaker.

Your strength and stature is rivaling their's they think, when you're not a rival at all, just in sync.

This the narcissist has built a life on your respondings to their promptings when you don't, they leave.

He's the puppetmaster: when you don't respond to his promptings it's a massive ego blow darling.

TO THE LOVE ADDICT

React or bye-bye: You have to be reactionary for the narcissist to feel his diabolical fulfillment.

Every time he dumps you and you come crawling back the soul tie hardens/he has more power: fact.

You can lay a boundary with a narcissist but he'll immediately bust it with no respect for it.

They have a hidden idealization [of selfhood] that sets up the criticism they're known for, it's there.

NECESSARY VULNERABILITY

Vulnerability--the hallmark of a good friendship--scares the narcissist to death, they can't have it.

The narcissist feels entitled: "I'm special, the rules that apply to you don't to me so get used to it girl".

Deep conversations with the narcissist are impossible. Tho' intelligent it's all breadth but no depth.

Say something about your life and he'll hijack the conservation to him, that's the way it is.

Only fake churches welcome Biden's move to expand abortions, real ones are sickened by him.

It's no longer pro-choice or abortion it's "women's reproductive rights", an evil euphemism.

Trans rights for bathroom more important than women's rights to privacy without men walking in.

Why are women's rights less important than trans-rights? Cuz the goal is NO gender/a unihuman type.

There is no self-awareness/education, the grooves in their brain are purely socially-determined.

SOCIAL PSYCH: CONTAGIOUS HATE

After just 4 years of Nazi affluence, they were ready to do to jews all what Hitler wanted/they perished.

EVIL FREAKS

Social Psych: In six years they went from friendly relations with Jewish neighbors to turning em in.

I grew so afraid of my German neighbor, what I call an "evil helper" causing me trouble with others.

Everything she thought was socially determined, nothing she came up with herself, shallow and cruel.

Every culture is different in their threshold levels beyond which novelty is taboo even violence too.

She wanted to "help" me but was running around to all the neighbors in her smear campaign/treachery.

The fat liberal females loved to hear the smears so got together in a small town soul-massacre.

They accused me of the very things they were doing but I'd never do, my good deeds called evil too.

SMALL TOWN SCAPEGOATISM

Small town angry frustrated fat females in the hot desert getting rid of their tensions on the target.

So I left Borrego for the desert wilderness to live in a ghost town and STILL they followed me out.

They would not leave me alone, the fat female pagan jealous jezebel calumnious broads of Borrego.

If in a city I'd never see the same person twice but closed in a small town it's a daily irritant like lice.

It was a liberal town in a blue state--that explains the social system of hate: Social Psychology.

Those 31 years dealing with groupies wrote these books on social psychology so I got off easy.

Now I'm in the opposite matrix: ingrown households on plots of land minding their own business.

The Nazi women were an equally or more perverted part of the Holocaust machine as were the men.

Atrocities by women in war are hard to quantify, running opposite to the image of women before.

WOMEN THE BEST PRISON GUARDS

Women took a very active role in the Holocaust. Many young women surpassed male sadists.

We are lucky to live in peacetime--on our own soil at least. Most lose it all/become least.

What I feared most was groupthought, for you aren't an individual but a category and you've had it.

Shame-based is all about what "they" think. You should be more based in Self cuz people are finks.

Most of their sour reactions to you were based on jealousy only, though you felt naughty.

You take it personally cuz toxic shame is passed down--it's genetic, a means of survival of mobs.

You've gotta transcend all this childhood stuff and find your SELF then toxic shame will be fluff.

Her sisters were jealous of her so she was ashamed about every little thing in her looks and personality.

TRANSCEND EARLY RESISTANCES

I was too big for original system, they didn't know about what I was talkin' and they were shunning.

EVIL FREAKS

Transcend early resistances to full potential and you come into the light surrounded by good-fellows.

It was so dark being in a system that didn't understand me nor want to try, disdaining all novelty.

Survivors said the most frightening thing was being seen as subhuman. I'm sure you can relate man.

He tends not to ask truly interested follow-up questions or next level comments, it's all about him.

THEY TURN ON ALLIES EASILY

Narcissists tend to turn on allies very easily. Once you're out he will walk right by you unseeingly.

The minute they broke up he never acknowledged her existence again, that's how it is with them.

Knowledge is power: The more you KNOW the more you say NO to these little signs, bringing growth.

The more you know the more you live in your healthiness as separated from their unhealthiness.

Anger is a major problem so learn to avoid a codependent dance taking you way down into a ditch.

Frustration is anger, it's on a spectrum--a warning sign tapping into your need for self-preservation.

ANGER STYLES THE INDICATOR

In ANGER you're standing for your worth as a human being--disrespect causes your agitation.

Anger prompts us to stand for our legitimate needs. Would you acknowledge them, please?

At times its your Core Convictions that are at stake. Anger prompts us to stand for these ok?

Anger is your emotion of self-preservation standing for your worth as a human and it's urgent.

Once seeing anger is a function we study anger styles and it is these indicating narcissism.

When annoyance/frustration/agitation is suppressed due to fear [of the narcissist] it's deadly dear.

His low empathy, haughtiness, entitlement: and I don't care what you think he adds, THREATENED.

The openly aggressive style is a strong narcissist. Once you see it you either truckle or ditch the dis.

PASSIVE AGGRESSIVE DIRT BALLS

The third style of anger management is the passive-aggressive: he strikes after hiding it.

Passive-Aggressive is obscure/evasive but angry at your expense: not showing up/making you wait.

The passive-aggressive is unreliable, changes his/her mind, withholds, makes mistakes, gossips.

They procrastinate, constantly sabotaging things tho' quiet, causing dissension while denying it.

I'd fear the passive-aggressive more than the loud and clear cuz it's the secret dangers from peers.

The jealous maid passive-aggressively leaks to the street about every little thing and it's irritating.

Passive-aggressive envious maid makes ageist remarks: just one word = incendiary sparks.

EVIL FREAKS

Everything is behind the scenes, they lack vulnerability to expose their true thoughts and feelings.

Traitors are insiders, always secretive with true feelings hidden but with the chance out they come.

After Wife of the Alcoholic Syndrome I was alone for years then Ray saved me from my peers.

Peers tend to come around if you're alone, unprotected. Sometimes I settled for less though elected.

I HATED THEIR COMPANY

I hated their company. Only a chosen mate can be in agreement, the others were dysynchrony.

Marriage gave me immediate protection from my peers. What freedom, at last! I now had a future.

You find a mate with whom you're in agreement then together you fight the world: it's perfect.

I had nothing but treachery from my peers. It'd be ok for awhile then they'd do something weird.

You're not fine-tuning a friendship like you would a mate. It can be aggravating to the first rate.

I just want you and me, me and you. Not a bunch of officious interlopers dropping in too.

I don't have the time for all those superficial relationships. I wanna know God and my destiny--no hicks.

LOW TRUST LEVELS

Narcissists have low levels of trust because if that vulnerable they lose control too much.

Healthy people recognize there will be conflicts but handle it with cleanness, civility and decency.

They are secretive as the only way to win, they've an inability to bond since that's too trustin'.

You can learn about people by studying how they handle conflict esp. when their needs are unmet.

Anger is a window into the internal spirit. It's significant since it's the false self which rears up.

It's all about filtering that social image to maintain their power base of self-absorbed preferences.

The less you know the less accountability they have to you and in their mind the better off they are.

Thought I'd lose my mind in a tiny town so moved way out to a ghost-town and here they came again.

BEGINNING OF THE END: APEX

There's a big distinction between the end and the beginning of the end which is your apex.

I'm at the top of my game but not to them, they only see numbers--don't let this discourage you sir.

It's extremely hard to lay privacy boundaries: just cuz you want it compels them to invade it see.

My privacy needs compelled their vicious gossip about what I might be doing--a red light district?

The liberal has a dirty mind and he projects it onto you the innocent target when it's all about HIM, aye.

I wrote the books on the problems with getting privacy, even non-interruptive office hours, no way.

EVIL FREAKS

THOSE IN POWER MAGNIFY IDEAS

Power magnifies the ideas of those who hold it. Previous to 1933 anti-semites weren't that regarded.

When minority gets in power evil becomes bloated--an example is Harris/Biden tho' we never chose it.

As a minority becomes enormously powerful their unacceptable beliefs become more acceptable.

Power magnifies the ideas of those who hold it. Think Biden/Harris then become the resistance.

If the economy flourishes in the 30's then they're happy with the Nazis and disdain the Jews see.

Every time they advanced east for living space millions more jews were added/deaths increased.

What Nazi Germany proved is things can change and they can change fast. Take nothing for granted.

Studying the Holocaust shows us the results of unchecked hatred and the fragility of society.

CHRISTIANS ARE HATED FOR LINES

Christians are hated for drawing lines. Boundaries: it's NO-NO-NO--the wicked hate that, aye?

There's nothing self-righteous about me. I'm a sinner like everyone else but I know my savior, see?

You'd prefer a God-hating atheist to a self-righteous Christian, are you kidding--are you serious man?

You'd prefer an atheist who accepts all degrees of immorality not a decent Christian hating treachery?

59

EVIL FREAKS

Yah, cuz you wanna do what you wanna do you hate the Christian who's always saying NO to you.

Atheist looks at sunset and doesn't SEE God. He's ungrateful for what He's made/he hates the rod.

God made you and gave you life and destiny. But you'd prefer a God-hater to a lover of Big Daddy?

I'm shocked at what I'm hearing from you. You seem like Satan's crew and your future looks blue.

Stick with God and you're always in the right. But side with God-haters and you've given up the fight.

NARCISSISTS CAN'T SELF-CORRECT

It's sad: a narcissist who can't listen or self-correct since he's the one but he will hit bottom, heck.

The narcissist is everywhere and it's all HIM. Therefore this is the generation of hatred of humble Christians.

Don't you dare tell the narcissist there's anything above HIM. Thinking that way he's destined for ruin.

Finally nothing can get me cuz I have a house, land, a wall w/locked gate and a husband to protect me.

This was an achievement of a lifetime: realizing I didn't need the world's approval just that ONE.

If that chosen ONE says I'm ok and it's ok what I do, if he approves of me--then to you all: fruit you.

Marriage is coming within a wall and if I turn off this computer all you out there don't exist at all.

I HATE THE PHONE/EMAIL ONLY

EVIL FREAKS

You wanna get me outa my home, inviting me here and there and you're SO offended I don't use phones.

You're offended I won't talk on the phone cuz I hate it, that I won't connect, that I prefer email instead.

You tell em about me then you run back telling me what they say and I'm telling you: GET OUT, today.

What the heck did people do before phones? They corresponded beautifully using artistic pens.

Don't be so naive to think you're not being influenced by the maid, the window washer, the gardener.

I don't want ANYONE in my house. I'll clean it exquisitely myself then no more Dunning-Kruger advice.

I see the new glycation baby/I can't stand it honey you've changed a bunch-- it's changed your archetype.

Fast for three days then go on fruits, yogurt, miso soups, rice, spuds and get that slaughterhouse outa you.

Those wrinkled extremities are from toxic acid crystals--FATTY acids/brown spots coming up: detox!

You can't tell him a thing, he knows it all even while he falls and it's a terrifying thing in front of us all.

The whole thing about mankind is it's saying it's good. It's always a veneer, a facade when really a hood.

I never said I was a holy angel, I've been around the block. I gave up on myself and chose highest: God.

COVER HER SINS NOT GOSSIP ABOUT EM

WOMEN: You're suppose to COVER her sins not shout em from the rooftop to anyone who'll listen sis.

You shouldn't be talking about sex anyway. You should be talking about staying alive/survival/family.

Study the Holocaust, see what can happen, broaden yourself and you won't be stressing this crap.

All those dry empty years in desert wilderness were NOT inefficacious, I was brewing underneath ashes.

All I can say after hearing you is "wrong stressors". I'm all mixed up/don't like and want back in my cage.

All those years muted by denial and fear were brewing for my future when it'd all spill out right here.

The inner RAGE I couldn't explain when being accused or misunderstood as something so inane.

The inner rage at being treated like a thing, like I didn't exist, like I had no feelings or reason to be pissed.

I couldn't explain this inner rage and to even express it made me afraid but I broke thru at an older age.

What changed this? Finding my SELF--talents, desires, tendencies, limitations--and boundaries UP.

What is home? PROTECTION from the [human] elements so what is the worse thing? Homelessness.

KINGS AND SULTANS FALL/ARE KILLED

Anytime you put God status on yourself you're destined for ruin. How to be big: be small and get smaller.

You crossed a line, they're starting to talk/exchange notes so your next slip-up will be seen as a crime.

First I had to see how much I suffered with people around with the mixed signals/jealousy triangulations.

EVIL FREAKS

Then I saw how I had to lay boundaries and enforce them. Once I mastered that I was in daily heaven.

It's hard being a Youtuber. They love you then they hate you then talk to the others and it's all over.

Great minds discuss ideas, avid minds discuss events, small minds discuss people. Eleanor Roosevelt

Small minded gossips are comfortable with mediocrity, talk about people, criticize their ideas/innovations.

She talked only about people she'd met but was never, ever interested in what's in MY head.

TO BE GREAT

I got so sick of hearing about people I had to cut the connection, too empty-headed ya' know.

To be great in this world you must do a Creative Act not chat on an on about who you've met you fake.

You must accomplish or create something, not chat yourself up/lie about credentials, boasting.

To be great, create--not promote yourself by Who You Know or pictures with powers you respect.

To be great you must be unique not rephrase others or plagiarize but boldly state what YOU think.

As I look back I feel only sadness from the results of a life so boundary-less and the influence of sadists.

From being a sitting duck to rigid control of everything I meet so it's not just luck, I've got my back.

THEY SENSED I WAS SMARTER

63

EVIL FREAKS

They sensed I was smarter so were compelled to bring me down and it took decades to truly understand.

I will not and cannot let your belittling disrespectful words hurt me anymore, you're a frenemy of my core.

For where envying and strife is there is every evil work. James 3: 16

Avoid jealous people because they trivialize accomplishments and minimize endeavors.

Interesting fact: States with most pornography have most plastic surgery as wives compete with teens.

Why should an accomplished woman in her 50's compete with a little nobody? But that's the way it is honey.

Fact: If someone's in my life I tend to take their bloody advice! They cost me greatly more than twice.

The wrong people will misadvise and you'll end up losing possessions and control, it's just no good.

Take the advice only of your spouse--they are the chosen ones and relying on their intuition is right/just.

If God's in your union He'll infuse it with wisdom and you will see that one plus one equals 20,000.

Fearing success: these are vain imaginations of bad when everything is going ok and that's PTSD.

If she shares secrets about other people sweetie I'm sure she's sharing yours with ease: female treachery.

If roots don't go down deep we live shallow and frustrated and get vindictive-- and then stuck.

BETRAYAL-TRAUMATIZATION

EVIL FREAKS

The betrayal-traumatized can't fight anymore--it's like they've been in a war, PTSD and more

I can speak from the heart in poetry cuz that's safe. After going thru trauma I can't speak any other way.

Only poetry and mathematics is safe. Tho' I love history it makes me feel crazy seeing human destiny.

My foundation/roots are very deep from decades of work, study and restless sleep overcoming sheep.

30 years solitude: avoiding culture as it was changing/building strength to come back again.

Crying out for help. I wanna come out but am totally stuck. Can't risk another hurt: PTSD does that.

Most don't know who they are, no identity just false self vs. me, a strong foundation from years on the cliff.

I've been traumatized so I can't risk ridicule, debasement or trivialization and that's why I'm locked in.

100% APPROVAL BY EVERYONE

If I don't have 100% approval forget it. If I'm not number one to everyone in the world, forget it/I mean it.

How ironic God would put a female writer thru trauma and mental illness in order to write all about it.

Cats are so special, don't you DARE speak against women and their adorable furry friends. We love em

Let's just say he clicked on the wrong thing. But with computers there's a record of it unfortunately.

PTSD AND UNHAPPY MEMORIES

EVIL FREAKS

PTSD memories warp our talent, grey our days, waste precious time, destroy our moods: NOT OK.

You can be so happy then without warning an unhappy memory intrudes. That's PTSD and you?

I can't reach out to you, sorry. I can't tell you what's in my heart, sorry. I can now only speak thru poetry.

PTSD bad memories totally ruin happiness in your present situation which would be so beautiful, amen.

I've gotta get off this event 35 years ago. The perpetrators are either dead or don't think of it at all.

They gripe and brawl over memories of ONE event for their entire lives. If mixed with alcohol, so dangerous.

Resolving/diluting bad memories is a symbol of being unstuck, finally transcending the guck.

I had audacity before this. I spoke my mind to audiences but after trauma it seemed too dangerous.

I can write poli-psych quips but I can't tell you what I feel. I can't take a chance, you could be a heel.

DUNNING-KRUGER LOSERS

I was attacked/imposed on by a buncha Dunning-Kruger losers for years and had MUCH to learn.

Music, dogs, cats, pretty views in total solitude while being protected in another house by some dude.

The female genius ends up talking in poetry or she doesn't talk--a logical adaptation to social blocks.

Short and sweet before their argumentations intervene, that's how we do it after all we've learned.

EVIL FREAKS

If you're getting creepy how am I suppose to love ya honey? There's something in ya/baloney.

Don't fruitin' come to my house imposing this stuff on me! That includes people too, get some class see.

AVOID CREEPY AND DARK

If there's anything creepy or dark I will withdraw. Please remember that darling as we go on.

You look like you're dying at times. Tho' you spring back I see the negative potential/am alarmed.

You can look really good or back--both extremes. It's alarming baby, gotta get some consistency.

I have limited time so waste none of it. Relaxation R & R isn't waste it's deserved/necessary rejuvenation.

The would-be genius has incapacity for leisure. Not me, I get into it every minute, it's how I work.

I don't know if you can be saved you seem really far gone but thru Christ such miracles are performed.

THIS IS SATAN, DON'T LET HIM

I'm freaked out by PTSD memories. Embarrassing, haunting, humiliating...this is Satan certainly.

To STAND means you're not moved by what's not changing. Joes Osteen

I study history and write. That's my life all day and night distracting me so I don't have to fight.

Attacked by a gang of boys and cops stood down. Tho' I've PTSD from this I'm still renowned.

Folks, fear God and Him alone. Fear man and it's just a snare. Pastor Charles Lawson

67

FAMILY SCAPEGOATS

My sister was the golden child and I was the scapegoat. This setup drove me mad, I hated the home.

To be cast in a bad light no matter what I did was the height of frustration and I sought escape.

They put me down to the world until everyone I met was primed against me. This is family treachery.

My two older sisters were the instigators. For decades they kept this game going as gossipers.

How narcissists treat their families: First she killed her husband, then mom, then my reputation see.

She banished him from his children and home in the most cruel way and he died in a desert trailer, ok

In my case I literally had to outlive my tormenters to get anywhere. Dysfunctional systems are a scare.

Massive Stockholm Syndrome as the victim starts to kiss up rather than fight. That's also PTSD alright?

She banished me too but it's all-ok cuz God placed me in another family right away, as He promised.

These sick systems only listen to each other keeping the fire burning, never individually discerning.

Only an ex-scapegoat can describe the horror of a big blank wall coming against you, whew.

THEY LAY EVIL SEEDS

The things they said about me were unbelievable. They planted evil seeds wherever I went, horrible.

What is a coward? Someone who has cowered.

EVIL FREAKS

These were my own sisters, so believe me families can be filled with such treachery and tragedies.

Their ends were not good. One was amputated then died and the other ended up insane besides.

My great family now is a husband, two dogs and five cats and that's ok—home is wherever love's at.

Are you pandering to youth or bringing them up? Are you conforming—uncouth--or growing up?

That's all I gotta say, I hope that's it for today but as the ready pen of a writer I'm on call 24/hrs a day.

JEALOUS WOMEN

Jealous women have tried to destroy me my whole life. I say this to young ladies: hold your head up high.

Moral of the story: If we don't forgive despite the horrific things they did then our body takes the hit.

Both Paul and Job lament the loss of wealth--there is no prosperity but they still love God/deny self.

Writing 130 books on Social Psychology was hard work and the only legacy I am leaving the earth.

That overwhelming feeling of chemistry could be a trauma bond or fatal attraction so I'd say watch & see.

The biggest obstruction to female genius is the female community itself--a crazy henhouse I kid you not.

When a woman targets you you've had it cuz she'll assiduously keep you in focus too.

When I relocated they planted evil seeds ahead of me, reduplicating the original system you see.

EVIL FREAKS

My in-law said I was sensitive that's why they hated me, my mom's friend said it was obviously due to envy.

It's not the end but the beginning of the end which is your APEX, what you've wanted all of your life.

Jesus removes *stain* of sin--what a miracle that is. Our past literally becomes white as snow: I'm in.

RELIEVE THE PRESSURE: FAST

To make the skin go taut, relieve the digestion from being bogged down then it snaps into a puppet.

To pull taut like a puppet go on juices for awhile or fast--relieve the lower energies of heaviness

My body told me long ago "too much digestion". Burping, acid reflux, choking was clear indication.

TV preachers like Osteen/Copeland are more new thought metaphysical and progressive Christianity.

Collagen and psyllium are my only two daily supplements cuz it's all about being glowing, fit, clean, slim.

At a certain point you lose your appetite/can't eat as much and that's when you need psyllium husks.

Glycation can be reversed I don't care what you say Mister--just go low fat and wait as it recedes further.

EVIL FREAKS

(Beyond Gross)

Horrors of a Borderless World

Everything you need to fulfill your destiny is already lined up—but can be lost or warped by other people who mess up.

I lived in bliss in the desert wilderness. But whenever someone would come to my home it was horrendous!

I hated arrivals and suffered for days. They were brazen, petty, grabby, mean or even obscene--the herd, ok?

I couldn't believe how sick people were. Well later I discovered it was a liberal town of gross sinners.

SINS SHOUTED FROM ROOFTOPS

Gross sinners behind closed doors but as you know sins are shouted from the rooftops as in Sodom Gomorrah.

Filthy sinners all of em, even little old ladies. Do you ever hear any mention of morality? Makes em angry.

The things they talk about are simply beyond gross. There are no more lines or boundaries, anything goes.

Severe undertow in human relations: If you don't stand up and demand the higher way, you're done.

My website begins with extreme austerity then opens up to discovery all about human destiny vs. this human tragedy.

EVIL FREAKS

As the Creative Act naturally completes itself like all of nature, everything miraculously comes together.

So you're a registered democrat, what crap! The party of infanticide, open borders, justice warrior brats.

They don't know what to think or what they're talking about and these people are running things.

Stop resentments from the past. You were weak--had you been strong they'd never act like that.

I was so weak/steeped in sin I didn't even know they were invading, just be a good hostess smiling.

There is a narrow gate that goes to heaven and a broad gate that SAYS "heaven" but goes to hell.

I put all past actors in a bag to throw out. That's my WWII, my bootcamp in what I now know about.

PEOPLE DIE BUT THE CREATIVE ACT REMAINS

People have come and gone and many have died. What has remained is the Creative Act applied.

Instead of old resentments acting like pin pricks I put em all in a bag called "my Ph.D. in the Streets".

I was like a slave faced with the illogic of the master and his double-binds as the culture declines.

Sick freaks beyond gross are everywhere and we've normalized it all-- it's all opposite to God.

I was angry at the lack of justice in liberal environments, or for sinful things their extreme tolerance.

EVIL FREAKS

SILENCE IS GOLDEN

Silence is golden because words have so much power. Words conger up bad visions and disempower.

She talks too dam much and your having to reply keeps you boring and down. It's better to be alone.

It's good to have friends but you don't have to sleep with em! Draw lines, be decent, down with liberalism.

The superior man lives the cycles of nature but to get there he completely separates from social bores.

A social life with agendas completely separates you from the abundance of nature and it's daily cycles.

There was no reasoning with her and she'd talk right through me as the narrative came first.

It's ALL social: names, fames, games, who they know, where they sit in the hierarchy: all your foes.

The feminist is so reversed from her naturalness she holds to a ridiculous line of reasoning tho' it's obvious.

I know, I had two older sisters, mother and several aunts all feminist and the only men were betas, victimized.

The men would lock themselves in rooms to avoid brawling angry women knocking on their doors all day.

And then when the two older angry liberal sisters got ahold of me that was the end of my life for decades.

SHIFTING ALLIANCES

How were the feminists ruthless when they had control? By gossiping constantly about me, that's all.

EVIL FREAKS

And then my mother, normally traditional, went on their side just to have 2 in her camp not just one.

My dry decades under the ruthless control of feminists was the dreary phase of the Heroines Journey.

But it all made me who I am today and overcoming tragedies is a soul beautifier ultimately.

Every decision feminists made was socially-driven, out of grace, stupid, counterproductive leading to ruin.

Having no boundaries God put me in a system where I had to lay them down fast or be overwhelmed.

You've reached a point where everyone around must be a confirmer. Sounds like the way of dictators.

If music evokes thought and writing then put it on. It's not just entertainment but vital to your setup.

To take someone's virginity is to "break a throne" and its indeed that since power comes from restraint.

You may as well surrender, you're hope is getting slender--that's what they all say so avoid em today.

Antifa profiling you as a "nazi" means your life is no longer sacred and your death unworthy to be mourned.

Well I won't put up with it for a minute, and I don't have the same problems others do so messed up.

Don't let em in, make em leave, return to home base which is SELFHOOD, alone, happy in nature's cycles.

WHERE IS ENLIGHTENMENT

You ALWAYS feel so much better after they've left. After three days they smell like fish--the guests.

74

EVIL FREAKS

TRUST the science: don't question us. That's called a "cult" and it's becoming bloody ridiculous.

It turns out it's better to start with music not end with it as a reward for working all day. INSPIRING, ole.

It's a SPIRIT unleashed onto the public of that era. Like touching the crotch by popstars in America.

That collective spirit is so strong one must be superstrong to avoid it while weakness falls into/emulates it.

Like having a whole mob twerking in obnoxious perversions suddenly--this is the collective spirit of insanity.

YES--always put the music on FIRST. It inspires me to the heavens and beyond, for music I've a thirst.

The bible talks of the fate of being ruled by children. Evil brats with no brakes--keep em out, put em away.

There is NO reasoning with them and the schools are propounding evil but I pray you don't succumb.

The evil brat stage sometimes lasts into middle age and beyond. Look at the woman those catty broads.

WHAT THEY'VE PUT US THROUGH

It's disgusting what they've put us through. Their constant tirades and demands for respect: pooh.

We all have our own way of expressing it. I find your way a bit puerile/sophomoric/obvious but I won't say it.

The genius must go solo. Everybody is a dam hindrance at this point but then there's management ya' know.

Like people "dropping by" using you as a pit stop--can there be anything more irritating, nope.

EVIL FREAKS

I'm telling you it's about impossible to get privacy. Get a mountain cabin and even then someone drops by.

Women are expected to attend to others, so if you want privacy or seem self-absorbed you're a target.

They WILL NOT let a woman have delicious wonderful otherworldly privacy--no, they will not.

They knock on the door, they call, they cause trouble or ruckus: you must escape this chaos.

They knew I was unprotected way out there so showed up at midnight to have me fix em a Mexican dinner.

This didn't happen too often in wilderness but when it did it was so stress-inducing I was down for decades.

It was so stress-inducing that people could think they could use me that way, esp. that I caved.

After 30 years in that liberal environment I literally had to pick up and leave and now I'm so pleased.

A social life is a chaotic, sad, anger-driven world but it's veiled with niceness covering those wicked girls.

Someone says something and they all turn against one. It's so tribalistic that way, this life is no fun.

Female community is a brutal atmosphere of gossip and conformity to viewpoints and shifting targets.

Never apologize for just wanting to be alone with God. Worrying with social anxiety is a major fault.

Cast your care--all those memories of bad things you did--onto Jesus and He'll make em white instead.

EVIL FREAKS

THE PAST LOOKS SCARY

I'm scared to death of the past viewed with new eyes when I see how vulnerable I was in a haze.

I thank God every day I'm in a nice home separate from the guests with a locked gate in a brand new state.

Not only did I cut off everyone from my past I'm gonna cut you off too and just enjoy music/movies/docs.

Dad said: Just movies, music and your poetry Karen, don't warp your mind with what's currently happenin'

If there's too much competition I'm gone. I have a major filter when it comes to you sir: I'm number one.

If it was just online, it's not a relationship you have to "get over". Stop kidding yourself, he/she's a player.

How to work your land: Just walk around and add what is needed or remove what doesn't belong.

Hone everything down to Tucker/Hannity/Laura at night and leave the rest of the day for the creative.

Regarding your online "relationship": He's having sex with two people and hankering over his ex: realize this.

I agree with Dad: music is most evocative but the world brings me down, confuses me, tires me out.

EVIL FREAKS

In their attempt to homogenize everything into "one" it was injustice, forced social, communism.

Deep thought is prohibited, complex thought is confronted as evil, only the narrative of the people.

Liberals force their friends on you too--so you can't vet them but that's the most important!

You're not a superman you just work a little each day. It adds up! If diligent you achieve much, ok?

For He performs what He has planned for me.

Details matter to God. He gets involved with complexities/intricacies, doesn't like ambiguity/generality.

ENTER THE NEW SEASON OF FAVOR

Once you enter the new season of FAVOR God just keeps giving and giving forever--you stay here.

Today I get new lazer-beamed eyes after destroying em from decades in work of great complexities.

God thru me designs my day. Not interruption-to-interruption, it's not gonna be that way.

When nothing's happening: "It's just not my season yet. God hasn't turned on the engine yet".

I know what it feels like to be hated and persecuted so I treat VERY WELL those who aren't doing it.

ALL the lessons had to do with boundaries, cuz if it's just me there's success and no tragedies.

EVIL FREAKS

They hated me until female rock stars made it acceptable to have short hair even buzzcuts if you dare.

How much of your problem was a dam liberal doing what they do best: to cause you trouble?

Though you've passed on I recall your words and it's like you never died, they have so much worth.

Your words had great worth until you let those people into your life. Then you changed, affirming that guy.

SERMONS ON HELL OR SIN ARE HATED

Give sermons on hell and churches are empty, but to the believer it gives joy/certitude, believe me.

HELL is filled with people who admired Jesus--that is not enough.

Every time faith is tested and survives, you know you have a supernatural faith. John MacArthur

Evil gospel of accommodation: changing the gospel to suit the needs of the people, making it nil.

Paul had a belly full of false preaching accommodating sins and desires of the fallen vs. the true gospel.

A watered down gospel is no gospel at all. Love God by refusing to teach an accommodating gospel.

After being hit by false gospels they hate the true one since man loves his sins/wants to keep em.

The sinner is a narcissist--loving himself--so he loves the false gospel that God loves him despite all.

Sinners love prosperity gospels where they can have whatever they want just by voicing it.

The more false the preacher--accommodating sinners--the more money he makes: ridiculous.

False preachers won't chastise the sexually perverse. God hates this and they both are cursed.

You can have your mansions and Bentleys by rewarding perversities but God'll punish it, surely.

ACCOMODATIONS OF THE FALSE CHURCH

The more false the church the more accommodating to sinners and thus the more mega its members.

The God-loves-everyone-no-matter-what church gains massive members overnight, of course.

Being drunk is the absence of wisdom and the presence of foolishness and we should avoid it.

You therefore still had to learn the lesson and that's why thru hell you were passin' so now forgive em.

I was messed up with masses of resentments 'til i learned to put it ALL in a bag: my WWII to forget.

I went through all that with people using me because I was weak and needed that very lesson.

You're born into all this confusion, it takes a life to sort it out--but morality does it easily enough.

In the past thousands of things happened in error. Don't relive each one, it was just that [lower] era.

EVIL FREAKS

From where I sit the past (what I put up with) brings disbelief and horror--see it as bootcamp, get it?

The past is so horrifyingly different it is easy to relapse back into it in erratic attempts to fix it.

When something bad happened at 35 and you're still pistoff at 65 that's an obviously wasted life.

Life is in two stages, primitive vs. evolved. Accept your primitive stage as ridiculous then leave it off!

Put all noxious past events into a bag. Now throw the whole bag out so the present isn't a drag.

INNOCENT FISH IN MUDDY WATERS

An innocent fish in muddy waters--demons took control and you couldn't help what you uttered.

It's udderly ridiculous all the big fake boobs in a sick society going down with homos all around.

That's right--demons take control of weak vessels and you were their slave and THAT'S why we forgave.

A weak abused child, rejected and unloved--left for dead, so of course you sucked up to the bad.

A weak vessel fish swimming upstream gulping water and drowning--so you went along, not knowing.

It just isn't my season yet, I'll attribute the utter quiet to that.

You wanted this, the utter quiet now free of the noisy wicked--now turn to God your loving Champion.

You wanted this, freedom--not knowing you'd be all alone so now go to God the only Love you've known.

EVIL FREAKS

High wall/locked gate--but still thinking about all the things that happened invaded by bad fate.

They'll pull you limb from limb and steal everythin'--then make you targets by angering everyone.

An innocent fish in muddy waters--demons took control and you couldn't help what you uttered.

It just isn't my season yet, I'll attribute the utter quiet to that.

A weak vessel fish swimming upstream gulping water and drowning--so you went along, not knowing.

THE UDDER-LY RIDICULOUS

It's udderly ridiculous all the big fake boobs in a sick society going down with homos all around.

A weak abused child, rejected and unloved--left for dead, so of course you sucked up to the bad.

They're gross and crass why would you miss those in the past. Enjoy this moment, refinement at last.

"I just don't care anymore" is a stage as cultures decline into ruin: apathy or nihilism.

Women are becoming pugnacious and gross let alone shallow thinkers accepting the liberal narrative.

Word and faith or name-it-claim-it are Satanic but that's different from completion: the Creative Act.

Believe-receive and name-it-claim-it is different from justified remuneration and recognition for work done.

The fact is God put the notion in you to do this Great Work and now He'll champion it/make you first.

EVIL FREAKS

The Creative Act is God manifest on earth, accomplishing changes in the people/an answer to the curse.

God gives you the blueprint in great detail. Attention to detail marks Christian-built Europe.

God accomplishes thru his servants, co-creators of the Creative Act, an actual structure in nature.

The Creative Act has a beginning, a middle and an end. The exact link to success is also definitive.

COMPLETION OF CREATIVE ACT IS MATURITY

The END or completion of the Creative Act is also maturity or wholeness--we have perfected ourselves.

But now I see I had to go through all that, as proven by the sad fact I put up with the dam dirty rats.

Why did the lessons about borders, boundaries and personal integrity (not getting crazy) take a lifetime?

Anything can happen in leftist culture cuz it's all about lawlessness, getting even and extortion.

It was dangerous hanging out with those young liberals, they could have killed you--now seclude.

The women have become frightening. If not fat or very fat, they are weird, pugnacious or idiots.

As a biocomputer my reactions to liberals was extreme confusion, terror, frustration and sadness.

Extreme alienation is what I felt in liberal environments. Anger at virtue signaling or the prevalent faking.

EVIL FREAKS

As a youth I drank at the liberal environment--my mal-adaptation to confusion or bad friends.

I felt so devastated, the sky was always grey. How'd I know it was due to liberalism and that I was ok?

I felt so sad, how'd I know it was from adapting to liberalism? The things they believe in, devastating.

They weren't born that way it's just a lust-practice. LUST we must believe in and even see as supremist.

I ate at the liberal contradictions all around, an emotional illness dealing with the devil's crowd.

I had an emotional illness because I lived in an emotional wasteland and mental drought--how'd I know?

NO PRIVATE PROPERTY ALLOWED—MUST SHARE

No private property allowed--you must share everything. Don't cave to demands of friends/siblings.

When around liberals I was always afraid--because their reality was so wrong, horrible, callous.

I was so riddled with resentment once I got away and grew up, I just put em in a bag/threw it out,

What about Islam, is it a blight? Well, it's about the harsh punishments that keep us up at night.

People gabbing trying not to step on toes--so boring and you know it too that's why you're drinking.

Your wife is so boring and wrong, she's a democrat thinking that makes her caring, loving...HAH

EVIL FREAKS

Your husband is so boring acting like a cuck saying he's a feminist but not knowing what's up.

Your boring husband says he's a feminist by mimicking some silly leftist book he read acting pist.

If you stand for truth (drawing lines) she'll get all her friends against you even get you arrested too.

How boring and common: A husband says he's a feminist so she'll give in at night or not be pissed.

If you really knew what your spouse was like voting like that. It's a loving image though a dam rat.

How can you stand her? Don't you know what she stands for? She approves of despicable horrors.

LIBERAL FEMINISTS USE GOSSIP AS A RUDDER

The liberal feminist uses gossip and slander as a rudder to control so her friends get hostile and bold.

Remember people go crazy and sin due to demons inside of them so don't be TOO hard on em.

Then why do they sin and attract demons? It's all due to weakness so stay strong my son.

If you try to curb sin or bad associations the childish feminist will fire up friends to bring you down.

Women are horrible when not sweet little ladies or nurturing mothers-- when that all reverses.

I love watching "Dallas" cuz it's all about the 80's before all this happened, the utterly unimaginable.

85

EVIL FREAKS

If you dare slam sin they'll get an army against you--that's how very much they love their sins.

Living thru WWII--or investigating WWII--puts us in the same boat: life is very serious ya know.

Theresa Mae: another female leader who can't think, constrained by liberal narrative and virtue-signaling.

Trouble is an incubator for greatness--it pushes you into your purpose. Paula White

When finally mature you look back, aghast.

Scary lookin' female! I'd hate to have her mad at me since feminists are now into pugnacity.

WOMEN THINK IT'S GOOD TO BE FURIOUS

Women actually think they're SUPPOSED to be furious. So they become hateful witches, delirious.

I had to go thru it all: being almost-killed by losers/tyrants before I finally got a fence after having my fill.

Men want women, women have power over men. So men GIVE IN to the feminist liberal narrative!

If your wife is a dam rat, a democrat, she's a baby killer and wants open borders, ruining our culture.

She became morally corrupt from the company she kept. Transference of spirits, muddy waters.

Needy for love but corrupted by feminism, when you turn away she instantly has an affair and that's not ok.

EVIL FREAKS

And then as a cuck you warm up to both of them, to be modern? Pathetic--never speak to em again.

The most sick-making influence is the "be loving" "all is one" consciousness pervading everything.

I'm not rude for not letting you in, YOU are rude for coming without announcing yourself or even asking.

As a cerebrotonic, invading my privacy actually HURTS physically and it makes the brain totally crazy.

THE SOCIAL GENERATION EXPECTS

And not only did you invade my privacy you brought all your friends too: how inept/without a clue.

You are too high maintenance if I have to put up with all this stuff you bring. You should be a blank slate, ok

When you come to see me shut up about all your opinions or endless describin' cuz I got my own thing.

I don't even have a couch in the main room--we meet at the business table then they go home and I'm off.

Everyone is able to come here and get everything for free except citizens who pay more tax, you see?

ARREST CALIFORNIA GOVERNOR AND SANCTUARY CITY MAYORS, NOW!

DEMOCRATS: All God's Children includes MS-13 to these fiends.

If liberals take over they WILL go door to taking the guns and executing Trump-supporters and Christians.

EVIL FREAKS

White culture is the least racist in the world. Go to any other culture and they will all see it as normal.

When a man faces death or eternity he calls for Jesus and no one else.

RIDDING BAD MEMORIES: SYSTEMS THEORY

From your new maturity you look back in sagacity and see immaturity created tragedies--let it go baby.

Looking back you have only yourself to blame. It was a lower life phase and if you see that, memory's ok.

You just didn't know how to deal with grabby youngsters and even needed their approval, the lil' monsters.

Bad memories is really about blaming others for our own fault. It was a system and we brought it all on.

If you're weak the grabby monsters will take all they can get. Blame your weakness and the rest, forget.

You even begged for it, letting crazy drugged youngsters in who anyone sane would know not to.

The world will flow in on you if you're weak. Blame yourself, totally: shift bad memories to SELF, see?

Many drunks die of bad memories they can't get over. Systems Theory is the cure: you brought it on lover.

Systems Theory brings incredible relief. Now you're not owned by bad memories, an energy thief.

The world robs you if you let it so be strong and reject it: Self-induced tragedies are how we learn this.

EVIL FREAKS

Way to rid bad memories: Just keep saying you brought it on. See the system, see the system--that's all.

AUTOIMMUNE PROTOCOL (AIP)

I have a problem with fiber so it's FRUIT AND FISH. I put a few greens in my smoothie, that's it.

I hate being told to put veggies in my gut then in pain all day cuz it's like a bowl of nails and I'm wrecked up.

AIP: No curry or chile. Even cocktail sauce on shrimp makes me wanna die all day.

It's fruit and fish. With anything else my body turns on me. By instinct I know this is correct, I feel it deeply.

A few greens in smoothie, why would we need more than that? They like it cuza the dressings on top of it.

The female behind is supposed to be shaped like an apple not a pear.

Why is everything curried now: to hide the taste of Walmart (Chinese) chicken, smells like fecal.

Bread fish with coconut powder/flakes, herbs, arrowroot powder NOT soy oil and bread crumbs (Walmart).

Bible filled with fruit and fish. Also says bread but that's for those who can take it and not be killed dead.

When you became a vegan you threw me outa your life completely and now you finally see it sweetie.

With gut pain from the fast, always think: PAIN = BEAUTY, after a short transition you'll have joy again.

BACK TO STARCH

Back to starch. Can't relate to the plant fats at all now. Bread with honey, cereal with raisins, fast til mornin'

For special I have mashed potatoes with vegan brown gravy and peas and corn: how I adore.

I love popcorn for snack: it's very low glycation while chips are incredibly high with all that fat surroundin' em.

Popcorn cooked in just a little avocado oil with no butter or fats of any kind of coarse but I love the salt.

I've returned to my roots regarding food, just like my dad ate daily: Bread with honey/spuds with gravy.

It's what I ate as a kid every day. Our first dietary adaptations determine what we need today?

Can't relate to the fruit--it doesn't get the job done and so is superfluous. Just get the starch in the house.

Don't fix too much. Suddenly I'm averse to left-overs. Esp. if it's cooked with water, think of the spores.

I completely agree with John MacDougal. It's about the starch and little else! A few greens, sparse.

As a kid meat was delicious to me. But as I matured mentally I found my limitations emotionally.

What I feel in my heart and mind transcends how things "taste" to me. Very few get to this point I think.

When I ate/enjoyed meat I never related to it mentally. It was just there for me but then I woke up, see?

What you do when hungry as a kid? Made cereal/put jam or honey on bread. Quick/perfect MacDougal said.

EVIL FREAKS

I'm down to some bread every 24 hours. Can't get much more austere than that: glycogen soars.

Eat as much bread and honey as you want once a day or for best results every two or three days.

The bible gives category to meat-abstainers and I think it's basic to many hypersensitives, I just can't sir.

ADDENDUM

NO I don't smile. You mean showing teeth like a Cheshire cat looking so stupid like you? Fake style.

And another thing: I hate your name dropping or conflating yourself with superior others as if brothers.

Dems will burn down your cities and say you did it and if you object they'll send BLM to your house.

God had to plant me in a ghosttown all alone in order to separate from culture and that was my throne.

God gave me this work in 52,000 tweets so He'll also have the link to the new life above the rinky-dink.

A discovery doesn't tell you what to think, it triggers subconscious analogies which is: INSIGHT.

EVIL FREAKS

THOSE IN POWER MAGNIFY IDEAS

Power magnifies the ideas of those who hold it. Previous to 1933 anti-semites weren't that regarded.

When minority gets in power evil becomes bloated--an example is Harris/Biden tho' we never chose it.

As a minority becomes enormously powerful their unacceptable beliefs become more acceptable.

Power magnifies the ideas of those who hold it. Think Biden/Harris then become the resistance.

If the economy flourishes in the 30's then they're happy with the Nazis and disdain the Jews see.

Every time they advanced east for living space millions more jews were added/deaths increased.

What Nazi Germany proved is things can change and they can change fast. Take nothing for granted.

Studying the Holocaust shows us the results of unchecked hatred and the fragility of society.

RELIEVE THE PRESSURE: FAST

To make the skin go taut, relieve the digestion from being bogged down then it snaps into a puppet.

To pull taut like a puppet go on juices for awhile or fast--relieve the lower energies of heaviness

My body told me long ago "too much digestion". Burping, acid reflux, choking was clear indication.

TV preachers like Osteen/Copeland are more new thought metaphysical and progressive Christianity.

EVIL FREAKS

Both Paul and Job lament the loss of wealth--there is no prosperity but they still love God/deny self.

Writing 130 books on Social Psychology was hard work and the only legacy I am leaving the earth.

That overwhelming feeling of chemistry could be a trauma bond or fatal attraction so I'd say watch & see.

It's not the end but the beginning of the end which is your APEX, what you've wanted all of your life.

THE TRAUMA-CREATED ULCER

To rid remorse for being an ass in the past/outclassed give your body to sunshine, learn to rhyme, dust.

I cured an ulcer with honey. In a few days the perennial pain was gone and I was on my way.

Coughing, exhaustion, acid reflux, nausea: Could be an ulcer and I cured mine with honey.

For 20 years she ignored the signs of ulcer: coughing, acid reflux, exhaustion, nausea when hungry.

She avoided the test and the meds for all that time but when she finally got in line felt SO FINE.

The ulcer creates stomach ache between chest and waist--it's all from acid so block it quick.

I thought I'd die from the acid reflux, the coughing, the nausea when hungry but they went away.

With an ulcer there's false fullness anyway, so stop eating temporarily and lay in the honey.

Once I took the dreaded big pharma med I felt so light and happy instead, finally rid of acid.

Acid ulcers have far worse symptoms than side effects of proton inhibitors as I found out.

All but fruits & veggies creates acid so go easy on diet and heal quickly by staying alkaline.

Smoking & drinking also causes such gut ulcers since they're acid-making. Lay off these things.

An ulcer causes such false fullness its easy to limit meals to tabs of nutubutter or honey.

Twenty years I suffered daily with this ulcer when it should be looked at immediately see.

Lay on the nutbutter and honey, take your proton inhibitor at night, the ulcer heals alright.

Pomegranate juice is an acid but like all fruits it goes alkaline in the blood but watch/limit it.

There's acid fruits vs. acid from bad foods. Two different things, learn the theory dudes.

THE HERD IN WORDS
HIX POLITIX
HOW THEY RUINED US
JUST SKIP DINNER
LE FEMME AND THE COMMUNIST SPIRIT
LIBERAL CHAOS & ROT
LIBERAL DOUBLETHINK
LIBERAL GALL 1 & 2
LIBERAL SHOVE-DOWNS
LOCK YOUR GATE
MANUAL FOR SUPERIOR MEN
MODERN ART FROM HELL
MOSTLY FAKE
NOTES TO CHAMPS 1 & 2
OVERCOME FRENEMIES
PC MAKES US CRAZY
PEOPLE ARE CRUEL
PEOPLE PROBLEMS 1 & 2
PERSECUTED GENIUIS
POLI-PSYCH MYSTERIES
PRETENTIOUS SLOBS
QUEEN BEE
RETURNING TO FIRST NATURE
THE SCHOOLS SCREWED EM UP
SEASON OF TREASON
SEPARATE MEANS HOLY
SOCIAL HYPNOTISM
SOLITUDE SOLUTION
SUPERCILIOUS
TOAD TO PRINCE
TRIALS CYCLES
TRUMP VS. GROUP
TRUST IN TRASH
THE TRUTH ABOUT PEOPLE
UNDERHEANDEDLY CLEVER
WALK TALL WITHIN WALLS
WE'RE NOT ALL ONE
WINNERS SKIP DINNER
WORK OR SMERK
FEMALE POWER DRIVE
RED NEW DEAL

AUTHOR BIO

Karen Kellock Ph.D.

Ph.D Political Psychology, UCI 1976
Post-Doctoral: UCI Medical School
Department of Psychiatry
Grants NIMH, NIAAA

Ph.D. dissertation "A Systems-Theoretic View of Pathologic Interaction" made an early mark as the "Wife of the Alcoholic Syndrome". Postdoctoral research at UCI Medical, Dept. of Psychiatry on the systems surrounding pathology on NIMH and NIAAA federal grants: *The Contagion of Madness: The Psychology of Neurotic Interaction and Pathological Systems*. Therapy tool Therapeutic Playwriting introduced the play *Mary and Murv: Gruesome Twosomes in the Alcoholic Marriage*. She taught Abnormal Psychology and Pathological Systems Theory at UC and CSU campuses and developed "the Debris Theory of Disease" in five books and website: (www.karenkellock.org): *Champion Guides, Daily Fastarian, Just Skip Dinner, Arts of Paleo Fasting, Ageless Cornucopia. Manual for Superior Men* is a pick-it-up-anywhere book that you can't put down (20,000 Kellockialisms) and ever on your desktop it should be found (or this Ebook for superior wordsearch of new jargon).